EMMANUEL JOSEPH

Germany's Global Diplomacy, Justice, Aid, and Military Engagement

Copyright © 2025 by Emmanuel Joseph

All rights reserved. No part of this publication may be reproduced, stored or transmitted in any form or by any means, electronic, mechanical, photocopying, recording, scanning, or otherwise without written permission from the publisher. It is illegal to copy this book, post it to a website, or distribute it by any other means without permission.

First edition

This book was professionally typeset on Reedsy.
Find out more at reedsy.com

Contents

1. Chapter 1: Introduction to Germany's Diplomacy — 1
2. Chapter 2: Historical Context and Evolution — 3
3. Chapter 3: Multilateralism and International Cooperation — 5
4. Chapter 4: Germany's Human Rights Advocacy — 7
5. Chapter 5: Humanitarian Aid and Development Assistance — 9
6. Chapter 6: Germany's Military Engagement — 11
7. Chapter 7: Germany and the European Union — 13
8. Chapter 8: Germany's Role in Global Economic Governance — 15
9. Chapter 9: Climate Diplomacy and Environmental Leadership — 17
10. Chapter 10: Cultural Diplomacy and Soft Power — 19
11. Chapter 11: Challenges and Criticisms — 21
12. Chapter 12: The Future of Germany's Global Diplomacy — 23

1

Chapter 1: Introduction to Germany's Diplomacy

Germany's role on the global stage has transformed significantly over the past century. The nation's tumultuous history, from the devastation of two world wars to the division and subsequent reunification, has deeply influenced its diplomatic strategies. Modern Germany is a testament to resilience and transformation, emerging as a key player in global politics with a strong commitment to peace, democracy, and multilateralism. This chapter sets the stage by examining the foundational principles that guide Germany's foreign policy, laying the groundwork for understanding its approaches to justice, aid, and military engagement.

Central to Germany's diplomatic efforts is a commitment to multilateralism and international cooperation. The nation is a staunch advocate for a rules-based international order, emphasizing the importance of adhering to international law and collective decision-making. Germany's active participation in global institutions such as the United Nations, the European Union, and NATO reflects this commitment. These organizations serve as platforms for Germany to champion global causes, ranging from human rights to sustainable development.

Economic strength plays a pivotal role in Germany's foreign policy. As Europe's largest economy, Germany wields considerable influence in international economic forums, including the G7 and G20. This economic clout enables Germany to advocate for policies that promote global economic stability and equitable growth. The nation's success in balancing a strong industrial base with innovative technology and green energy initiatives further underscores its leadership in global economic governance.

Cultural diplomacy is another vital aspect of Germany's global outreach. Institutions like the Goethe-Institut play a crucial role in promoting German culture, language, and values worldwide. By fostering cross-cultural exchanges and supporting educational initiatives, Germany seeks to build bridges and strengthen international relations. This soft power approach complements its traditional diplomatic efforts, enhancing its global image and influence.

In conclusion, Germany's diplomacy is a multifaceted endeavor grounded in historical experience and contemporary global challenges. The nation's dedication to multilateralism, economic leadership, and cultural exchange reflects a comprehensive approach to foreign policy. As we delve deeper into Germany's diplomatic efforts in subsequent chapters, we will explore how these foundational principles translate into concrete actions and initiatives on the global stage.

2

Chapter 2: Historical Context and Evolution

Germany's diplomatic evolution is deeply intertwined with its tumultuous history. The aftermath of World War II left Germany in ruins, both physically and politically. The nation's subsequent division into East and West Germany during the Cold War further complicated its international standing. This chapter delves into how these historical events have shaped Germany's foreign policy, highlighting the nation's journey from a pariah state to a respected global leader committed to peace and cooperation.

Post-World War II, Germany's foreign policy was heavily influenced by its desire to rehabilitate its international image and prevent future conflicts. The establishment of the Federal Republic of Germany (West Germany) in 1949 marked the beginning of a new era. West Germany's integration into the Western bloc, through alliances such as NATO and the European Economic Community, was a strategic move to align itself with democratic nations and promote economic recovery.

The fall of the Berlin Wall in 1989 and the subsequent reunification of East and West Germany in 1990 were watershed moments in the nation's history. Reunification not only restored Germany's territorial integrity but also marked its full return to the international community. This period saw Germany embrace a more active role in global diplomacy, advocating for European integration and contributing to international peacekeeping missions.

Germany's diplomatic strategies during the Cold War were characterized by Ostpolitik, a policy aimed at improving relations with Eastern European countries and the Soviet Union. Ostpolitik, championed by Chancellor Willy Brandt, sought to ease tensions and promote dialogue between East and West. This policy laid the groundwork for Germany's modern approach to diplomacy, emphasizing dialogue, cooperation, and reconciliation.

In the post-Cold War era, Germany has continued to evolve its foreign policy to address emerging global challenges. The nation's commitment to multilateralism, human rights, and sustainable development has become increasingly prominent. Germany's historical experiences, including its division and reunification, have instilled a deep understanding of the importance of peace and cooperation. As we move forward, we will explore how these historical influences shape Germany's current diplomatic efforts in justice, aid, and military engagement.

3

Chapter 3: Multilateralism and International Cooperation

Germany's commitment to multilateralism is a cornerstone of its foreign policy. Rooted in the belief that collective action is essential for addressing global challenges, Germany actively participates in international organizations and initiatives. This chapter explores Germany's role in key international bodies, such as the United Nations, the European Union, and NATO, and its efforts to foster international cooperation and dialogue.

The United Nations serves as a crucial platform for Germany to promote its foreign policy objectives. As a non-permanent member of the UN Security Council, Germany advocates for international peace and security, human rights, and sustainable development. Germany's contributions to UN peacekeeping missions and its support for initiatives such as the Sustainable Development Goals (SDGs) underscore its commitment to multilateralism.

Germany's role in the European Union is equally significant. As one of the EU's founding members and its largest economy, Germany plays a leading role in shaping EU policies and initiatives. Germany's advocacy for European integration, economic stability, and solidarity among member states reflects its belief in the importance of a strong and united Europe. The nation's efforts to address issues such as migration, climate change, and security within the

EU framework demonstrate its dedication to collective solutions.

NATO is another key pillar of Germany's multilateral approach. As a member of this military alliance, Germany contributes to collective defense and security efforts. Germany's participation in NATO missions, such as those in Afghanistan and the Balkans, highlights its commitment to maintaining international peace and stability. Germany also actively engages in dialogue with non-NATO countries to promote cooperation and conflict resolution.

In addition to these major organizations, Germany is involved in various international coalitions and partnerships. The nation plays a leading role in the G7 and G20, where it advocates for global economic governance and sustainable development. Germany's efforts to build alliances and foster dialogue extend to issues such as climate change, digitalization, and global health.

In conclusion, Germany's dedication to multilateralism and international cooperation is a defining feature of its foreign policy. By actively participating in international organizations and building coalitions, Germany seeks to address global challenges through collective action. This commitment to multilateralism not only enhances Germany's global influence but also contributes to a more just and stable international order.

4

Chapter 4: Germany's Human Rights Advocacy

Germany's commitment to human rights is a central aspect of its foreign policy. The nation actively promotes human rights and justice on the global stage, drawing on its historical experiences and democratic values. This chapter examines Germany's efforts to champion human rights through international treaties, support for non-governmental organizations, and diplomatic initiatives.

Germany's dedication to human rights is reflected in its involvement in international human rights treaties and conventions. The nation is a signatory to key agreements such as the Universal Declaration of Human Rights, the International Covenant on Civil and Political Rights, and the Convention on the Elimination of All Forms of Discrimination Against Women. Germany's adherence to these treaties underscores its commitment to upholding human rights standards.

Support for non-governmental organizations (NGOs) is another vital component of Germany's human rights advocacy. The German government provides funding and resources to NGOs that work to protect and promote human rights around the world. Organizations such as Amnesty International, Human Rights Watch, and local grassroots groups benefit from Germany's support. This collaborative approach strengthens global human rights efforts and amplifies the voices of those fighting for justice.

Germany's diplomatic initiatives also play a crucial role in advancing human rights. The nation consistently advocates for human rights in international forums such as the United Nations Human Rights Council. Germany's diplomatic missions around the world engage in dialogue with local governments and civil society to address human rights concerns. Issues such as freedom of expression, gender equality, and the protection of minorities are central to Germany's diplomatic agenda.

Germany's historical experiences have profoundly shaped its commitment to human rights. The atrocities of the Holocaust and the repressive regimes in East Germany serve as stark reminders of the importance of protecting human dignity. Germany's efforts to confront and reconcile with its past have reinforced its dedication to promoting justice and human rights globally.

In conclusion, Germany's human rights advocacy is a testament to its commitment to justice and the protection of human dignity. Through international treaties, support for NGOs, and diplomatic initiatives, Germany strives to uphold and promote human rights around the world. This unwavering dedication to human rights not only defines Germany's foreign policy but also contributes to a more just and humane global community.

5

Chapter 5: Humanitarian Aid and Development Assistance

Germany is a leading provider of humanitarian aid and development assistance, reflecting its commitment to global solidarity and sustainable development. This chapter explores Germany's strategies for delivering aid, supporting development projects, and addressing crises around the world. The nation's efforts in areas such as disaster relief, healthcare, education, and infrastructure development will be examined in detail.

Germany's humanitarian aid initiatives are guided by principles of impartiality, neutrality, and humanity. The nation responds swiftly to natural disasters, conflicts, and other emergencies, providing essential assistance to affected populations. German humanitarian organizations, such as the German Red Cross and Welthungerhilfe, play a crucial role in delivering aid on the ground. Germany's contributions to international relief efforts, such as those coordinated by the United Nations Office for the Coordination of Humanitarian Affairs (OCHA), further underscore its commitment to alleviating human suffering.

In addition to emergency relief, Germany invests significantly in long-term development projects. The German Agency for International Cooperation (GIZ) is a key institution responsible for implementing development programs worldwide. GIZ's initiatives focus on areas such as economic development, education, healthcare, and environmental protection. By promoting sustainable development, Germany aims to address the root causes of poverty and promote stability in vulnerable regions.

Education is a key focus area for Germany's development assistance. The nation supports educational programs that aim to improve access to quality education, particularly in developing countries. Initiatives such as the German Academic Exchange Service (DAAD) provide scholarships and funding for students from around the world to study in Germany. By investing in education, Germany helps empower individuals and communities, fostering long-term development and social progress.

Healthcare is another critical component of Germany's development assistance. The nation supports global health initiatives, providing funding and expertise to combat diseases, improve healthcare infrastructure, and enhance medical training. Germany's contributions to organizations such as the World Health Organization (WHO) and the Global Fund to Fight AIDS, Tuberculosis, and Malaria are examples of its commitment to global health. By addressing health challenges, Germany aims to improve the well-being of communities and reduce health disparities.

Infrastructure development is essential for sustainable growth, and Germany invests in projects that enhance transportation, energy, and communication systems in developing countries. Germany's support for renewable energy projects, such as solar and wind power, promotes sustainable and environmentally friendly development. By investing in infrastructure, Germany helps create the conditions for economic growth and social development.

In conclusion, Germany's humanitarian aid and development assistance efforts reflect its commitment to global solidarity and sustainable development. Through emergency relief, education, healthcare, and infrastructure projects, Germany aims to support vulnerable populations and promote long-term stability. These initiatives not only address immediate needs but also contribute to the broader goal of building a more just and equitable world.

6

Chapter 6: Germany's Military Engagement

Germany's approach to military engagement is shaped by its commitment to peace and international cooperation. While the nation emphasizes diplomatic solutions, it recognizes the importance of military engagement in maintaining global security. This chapter explores Germany's role in international peacekeeping missions, its contributions to NATO, and its efforts to balance military engagement with diplomatic initiatives.

Germany's military strategy is characterized by its focus on defensive capabilities and international cooperation. The nation maintains a robust military force, the Bundeswehr, which is equipped to respond to a range of security challenges. Germany's military doctrine emphasizes the importance of multilateralism and collective defense, aligning its military efforts with broader diplomatic goals.

Germany's participation in international peacekeeping missions is a testament to its commitment to global security. The nation contributes troops and resources to United Nations peacekeeping operations, helping to stabilize conflict zones and protect civilian populations. Germany's involvement in missions such as those in Mali, Lebanon, and the Balkans highlights its dedication to maintaining peace and security worldwide.

NATO is a key platform for Germany's military engagement. As a member of this alliance, Germany plays a vital role in collective defense and security efforts. The nation contributes to NATO missions and exercises, enhancing its military readiness and interoperability with allied forces. Germany's support for NATO's strategic goals, including deterrence and defense, underscores its commitment to transatlantic security.

Germany's military engagement is not limited to traditional defense operations. The nation also focuses on addressing emerging security challenges, such as cyber threats and terrorism. Germany's efforts to enhance its cyber defense capabilities and collaborate with international partners reflect its proactive approach to contemporary security issues. By addressing these challenges, Germany aims to contribute to a safer and more stable international environment.

In conclusion, Germany's military engagement is guided by its commitment to peace and international cooperation. Through participation in peacekeeping missions, contributions to NATO, and efforts to address emerging security challenges, Germany strives to maintain global security while upholding its diplomatic principles. This balanced approach underscores the nation's dedication to creating a safer and more secure world.

7

Chapter 7: Germany and the European Union

Germany's role within the European Union is central to its foreign policy and diplomatic efforts. As one of the EU's founding members and its largest economy, Germany plays a pivotal role in shaping the union's policies and initiatives. This chapter explores Germany's influence within the EU, its efforts to promote European integration, and its contributions to addressing key challenges facing the continent.

Germany's advocacy for European integration is a cornerstone of its EU policy. The nation believes that a united and cohesive Europe is essential for addressing global challenges and promoting stability. Germany has consistently supported initiatives that enhance political, economic, and social integration within the EU. The nation's efforts to strengthen the EU's institutions and promote solidarity among member states reflect its commitment to European unity.

Economic policy is a key area where Germany exerts significant influence within the EU. As the largest economy in the union, Germany plays a leading role in shaping economic policies and initiatives. The nation's emphasis on fiscal discipline, economic stability, and sustainable growth has shaped the EU's economic agenda. Germany's support for initiatives such as the European Stability Mechanism (ESM) and the Banking Union underscores its commitment to ensuring the financial stability of the Eurozone.

Germany's stance on migration and refugee policies has also been influential within the EU. The nation has advocated for a comprehensive and humane approach to addressing migration challenges, emphasizing the importance of solidarity and shared responsibility among member states. Germany's efforts to support refugees and integrate them into society serve as a model for other EU countries. The nation's leadership on migration issues highlights its commitment to upholding human rights and promoting social cohesion.

Security and defense are other critical areas where Germany contributes to the EU's efforts. The nation supports initiatives aimed at enhancing the EU's collective security and defense capabilities. Germany's involvement in projects such as the Permanent Structured Cooperation (PESCO) and the European Defence Fund reflects its commitment to strengthening the EU's ability to address security challenges. By promoting cooperation and integration in defense matters, Germany aims to enhance the EU's role as a global security actor.

In conclusion, Germany's role within the European Union is characterized by its leadership and commitment to promoting integration, stability, and security. Through its influence on economic, migration, and security policies, Germany seeks to strengthen the EU and enhance its ability to address global challenges. This dedication to European unity and cooperation reflects Germany's broader diplomatic principles and its vision for a stronger and more cohesive Europe.

8

Chapter 8: Germany's Role in Global Economic Governance

Germany's economic strength gives it significant influence in global economic governance. As one of the world's leading economies, Germany plays a pivotal role in shaping international economic policies and addressing global economic challenges. This chapter explores Germany's participation in international economic forums, its economic policies, and its efforts to promote sustainable and inclusive growth.

Germany's involvement in international economic forums such as the G7 and G20 is a key aspect of its global economic governance. These forums provide platforms for Germany to advocate for policies that promote economic stability, trade, and development. Germany's leadership in these forums reflects its commitment to addressing global economic challenges through multilateral cooperation. The nation's efforts to promote fair trade, financial stability, and sustainable development are central to its economic diplomacy.

Sustainable and inclusive growth is a priority for Germany's economic policies. The nation emphasizes the importance of balancing economic growth with environmental protection and social equity. Germany's commitment to renewable energy, green technologies, and climate-friendly policies reflects its dedication to sustainability. Initiatives such as the Energiewende (energy transition) aim to reduce carbon emissions and promote clean energy, setting an example for other countries to follow.

Trade is another critical component of Germany's economic governance. As one of the world's leading exporters, Germany advocates for open and fair trade practices. The nation supports the rules-based international trading system and works to strengthen institutions such as the World Trade Organization (WTO). Germany's efforts to promote free trade agreements and reduce trade barriers reflect its belief in the benefits of global trade for economic growth and development.

Development assistance is also an integral part of Germany's economic governance. The nation provides significant funding and support for development projects in developing countries. Germany's contributions to initiatives such as the Global Partnership for Effective Development Cooperation (GPEDC) and the International Development Association (IDA) highlight its commitment to promoting economic development and reducing poverty. By supporting inclusive growth and development, Germany aims to create a more equitable global economy.

In conclusion, Germany's role in global economic governance is characterized by its leadership and commitment to promoting stability, sustainability, and inclusivity. Through participation in international economic forums, advocacy for sustainable growth, support for free trade, and development assistance, Germany seeks to address global economic challenges and contribute to a more prosperous and equitable world. This dedication to economic governance reflects Germany's broader diplomatic principles and its vision for a more just and sustainable global economy.

9

Chapter 9: Climate Diplomacy and Environmental Leadership

Germany is a global leader in climate diplomacy and environmental protection. The nation has made significant commitments to combat climate change and promote environmental sustainability. This chapter explores Germany's efforts in climate diplomacy, its support for international climate agreements, and its initiatives to promote green technologies and renewable energy.

Germany's commitment to climate diplomacy is reflected in its active participation in international climate agreements. The nation is a strong supporter of the Paris Agreement, which aims to limit global warming to well below 2 degrees Celsius. Germany's efforts to reduce greenhouse gas emissions and promote climate resilience are central to its climate diplomacy. The nation's leadership in international climate negotiations highlights its dedication to addressing the global climate crisis.

Renewable energy and green technologies are key components of Germany's environmental leadership. The nation has made significant investments in renewable energy sources such as solar, wind, and biomass. Initiatives such as the Energiewende (energy transition) aim to increase the share of renewable energy in Germany's energy mix and reduce reliance on fossil fuels. By promoting clean energy, Germany sets an example for other countries and contributes to global efforts to combat climate change.

Germany's support for climate finance is another vital aspect of its climate diplomacy. The nation provides funding and resources to help developing countries mitigate and adapt to climate change. Germany's contributions to initiatives such as the Green Climate Fund (GCF) and the Global Environment Facility (GEF) reflect its commitment to supporting vulnerable countries in their climate efforts. By providing climate finance, Germany helps ensure that all countries can participate in global climate action.

Climate diplomacy extends beyond environmental policies to include broader sustainability initiatives. Germany extends its efforts to promoting sustainable urban development, biodiversity conservation, and resource efficiency. The nation supports initiatives that aim to create sustainable cities, protect natural ecosystems, and promote sustainable consumption and production patterns. Germany's engagement in international partnerships, such as the United Nations Environment Programme (UNEP) and the Convention on Biological Diversity (CBD), underscores its comprehensive approach to environmental sustainability.

Public awareness and education are also crucial elements of Germany's climate diplomacy. The nation invests in raising awareness about climate change and environmental protection, both domestically and internationally. Germany's educational programs, public campaigns, and support for research and innovation contribute to building a global culture of sustainability. By fostering a deeper understanding of environmental issues, Germany empowers individuals and communities to take meaningful action.

In conclusion, Germany's climate diplomacy and environmental leadership are marked by its commitment to international climate agreements, promotion of renewable energy, support for climate finance, and comprehensive sustainability initiatives. Through these efforts, Germany aims to lead the global transition to a sustainable future. The nation's dedication to climate action reflects its broader diplomatic principles and its vision for a healthier planet.

10

Chapter 10: Cultural Diplomacy and Soft Power

Germany's cultural diplomacy is a vital component of its global outreach, leveraging soft power to build relationships and promote its values. This chapter explores Germany's efforts to promote its culture and values through international cultural exchanges, educational initiatives, and support for the arts. The role of institutions such as the Goethe-Institut in fostering cross-cultural understanding will be examined in detail.

Cultural diplomacy serves as a bridge between Germany and the world, promoting mutual understanding and cooperation. The Goethe-Institut, Germany's cultural institute, plays a central role in this effort. With a global network of offices, the Goethe-Institut offers language courses, cultural programs, and artistic exchanges that highlight German culture and foster dialogue. These initiatives help build connections and enhance Germany's cultural influence.

Education is a key focus of Germany's cultural diplomacy. The nation offers a range of educational programs and scholarships that enable students from around the world to study in Germany. Initiatives such as the German Academic Exchange Service (DAAD) provide opportunities for academic exchange and collaboration. By supporting international education, Germany promotes cross-cultural understanding and strengthens global academic partnerships.

Germany's support for the arts is another crucial aspect of its cultural diplomacy. The nation funds and promotes a wide range of artistic endeavors, including music, literature, film, and visual arts. German artists and cultural institutions are active participants in international festivals, exhibitions, and collaborations. Through these efforts, Germany showcases its cultural richness and fosters artistic exchange.

Science and innovation are also integral to Germany's soft power strategy. The nation supports international scientific collaboration and research partnerships, promoting innovation and knowledge sharing. German research institutions and universities are at the forefront of global scientific advancements, contributing to solutions for pressing global challenges. By promoting scientific cooperation, Germany enhances its global influence and contributes to global progress.

In conclusion, Germany's cultural diplomacy and soft power efforts are characterized by a commitment to promoting its culture, values, and knowledge. Through international cultural exchanges, educational initiatives, support for the arts, and scientific collaboration, Germany aims to build bridges and strengthen international relations. These efforts reflect Germany's broader diplomatic principles and its vision for a more connected and understanding world.

11

Chapter 11: Challenges and Criticisms

Despite its achievements, Germany's global diplomacy faces various challenges and criticisms. This chapter explores the obstacles and criticisms that Germany encounters in its diplomatic efforts, including geopolitical tensions, domestic political pressures, and critiques of its policies. The chapter also discusses how Germany addresses these challenges and strives to uphold its diplomatic principles.

Geopolitical tensions pose significant challenges to Germany's diplomatic efforts. The nation must navigate complex international relations, including its interactions with major powers such as the United States, China, and Russia. Balancing these relationships while maintaining its commitment to multilateralism and international cooperation requires careful diplomacy. Geopolitical conflicts and regional instability also impact Germany's ability to pursue its foreign policy objectives.

Domestic political pressures can influence Germany's foreign policy decisions. Public opinion, political parties, and interest groups all play a role in shaping Germany's diplomatic priorities. Policy decisions, such as those related to military engagement or migration, can be contentious and subject to debate within Germany. Navigating these domestic pressures while adhering to foreign policy principles is a constant challenge for German policymakers.

Criticisms of Germany's policies also present challenges. Some critics argue that Germany's economic policies prioritize national interests over global solidarity. Others point to perceived inconsistencies in Germany's human rights advocacy, such as its relationships with countries with questionable human rights records. Additionally, Germany's military engagement and arms exports have faced scrutiny from both domestic and international observers. Addressing these criticisms and ensuring policy coherence is an ongoing task for Germany.

Germany's commitment to transparency and dialogue is key to addressing these challenges. The nation engages in open discussions with stakeholders, both domestically and internationally, to build consensus and address concerns. Germany's efforts to explain its policies, provide accountability, and seek input from various actors reflect its dedication to maintaining trust and credibility in its diplomacy.

In conclusion, Germany's global diplomacy faces a range of challenges and criticisms that require careful navigation and thoughtful responses. By addressing geopolitical tensions, domestic political pressures, and policy critiques, Germany strives to uphold its diplomatic principles and maintain its positive impact on the world stage. These efforts underscore Germany's dedication to transparency, dialogue, and the pursuit of a more just and stable international order.

12

Chapter 12: The Future of Germany's Global Diplomacy

As Germany looks to the future, it faces both opportunities and challenges that will shape its global diplomacy. This chapter explores emerging trends and issues that may influence Germany's diplomatic strategies in the coming years. The chapter also highlights Germany's vision for a more just, peaceful, and sustainable world and its commitment to adapting to changing global dynamics.

One of the key trends shaping the future of Germany's diplomacy is the rise of digitalization and technological advancements. As technology continues to transform societies and economies, Germany will need to navigate the implications for international relations. Issues such as cybersecurity, digital governance, and the ethical use of technology will be central to Germany's diplomatic agenda. Embracing innovation while addressing the associated challenges will be crucial for Germany's global leadership.

Climate change and environmental sustainability will remain at the forefront of Germany's diplomatic efforts. The nation will continue to advocate for ambitious climate action and support international agreements that address the climate crisis. Germany's leadership in renewable energy and green technologies will be pivotal in driving global efforts toward a sustainable future. Adapting to the impacts of climate change and promoting resilience will also be key priorities.

Global health and pandemic preparedness are emerging issues that will shape Germany's diplomacy. The COVID-19 pandemic has underscored the importance of international cooperation in addressing health crises. Germany will continue to support global health initiatives and advocate for strengthening health systems worldwide. The nation's contributions to vaccine distribution, research, and healthcare infrastructure will play a vital role in enhancing global health security.

Geopolitical shifts and changing power dynamics will also influence Germany's diplomacy. The rise of emerging powers, shifting alliances, and regional conflicts will require Germany to adapt its strategies and build new partnerships. Maintaining a balance between established relationships and engaging with new actors will be essential for Germany's diplomatic effectiveness. The nation's commitment to multilateralism and international cooperation will guide its approach to these evolving challenges.

In conclusion, the future of Germany's global diplomacy will be shaped by emerging trends and challenges that require adaptive strategies and visionary leadership. By embracing digitalization, addressing climate change, enhancing global health, and navigating geopolitical shifts, Germany aims to continue its positive impact on the world stage. The nation's commitment to justice, peace, and sustainability will remain central to its diplomatic efforts, guiding its vision for a better future for all.

Book description: "Germany's Global Diplomacy: Justice, Aid, and Military Engagement":

"Germany's Global Diplomacy: Justice, Aid, and Military Engagement" provides an insightful exploration of Germany's influential role on the international stage. This book traces the evolution of German diplomacy from a nation marred by the aftermath of two world wars to a leader in global politics committed to peace, democracy, and multilateralism.

Delving into the historical context, the book examines how Germany's past has shaped its current diplomatic strategies. It highlights the nation's commitment to multilateralism, showcasing Germany's active participation in international organizations such as the United Nations, European Union, and

CHAPTER 12: THE FUTURE OF GERMANY'S GLOBAL DIPLOMACY

NATO. Economic strength, cultural diplomacy, and the nation's dedication to human rights advocacy are core themes explored in depth.

Readers will gain an understanding of Germany's humanitarian aid efforts, which include disaster relief, healthcare, education, and infrastructure development. The book also provides a comprehensive overview of Germany's military engagement, balancing defensive capabilities with international cooperation to maintain global security.

Furthermore, the book addresses Germany's pivotal role within the European Union, its influence in global economic governance, and its leadership in climate diplomacy. Cultural diplomacy and soft power are also discussed, highlighting Germany's efforts to promote its culture and values worldwide.

Despite its achievements, Germany faces various challenges and criticisms, which are thoughtfully analyzed. The book concludes by looking to the future, discussing emerging trends and issues that will shape Germany's diplomatic strategies in the years to come.